THE HABIT PROJECT

9 Powerful Strategies to Build Habits That Stick

(And Supercharge Your Productivity, Health, Wealth and Happiness)

Akash Karia

www.AkashKaria.com

#1 Internationally Bestselling Author of
The 7 Things Resilient People Do Differently

Bestselling Books by Akash Karia

The 7 Things Resilient People Do Differently

How Successful People Think Differently

How to Deliver a Great TED Talk

How to Design TED-Worthy Presentation Slides

Free Resources

There are hundreds of free articles as well as several eBooks, MP3s and videos on Akash's blog. To get instant access to those, head over to www.AkashKaria.com/Habits.

RAVE REVIEWS FROM READERS

"One of the best books I've read in a long time..."
~ Hyrum

"I really enjoyed Akash Karia's *The Habit Project*. His clear breakdown of the process of habit formation, tools to overcome failure, and great examples to illustrate his points have inspired me to tackle a couple of habits on my wish list. Packed with strategies, this could be just the push you need to add a new habit to your routine, or cut a bad one from your life."
~ Sheila L. Gibson

"Crisp and clear."
~ Ramakrishna Reddy

"If there's one thing I appreciate about any Akash Karia books is that [they're] straightforward, no-nonsense, and [filled] with tips that you can apply after you finish reading the book...*The Habit Project* is a concrete example of how you can engineer your way to productivity and wellness."
~ Caleb Galaraga

"Intriguing read..."
~ William Bridges

"I really enjoyed reading this book! The author explains in great detail how habits work, and provides many examples to make the concept of "habits" easier to understand. He designed a "map" on how we can build new, healthier habits in our lives and he breaks the process down, step by step."
~ Claudia Svartefoss

"...to the point with great tips!"
~ Samantha

"I like when I read a book that actually has advice in it that I can use. Akash has written that book for me."
~ Michael Wilkinson

"Great book with great ideas."
~ Luis L.

"Fantastic book. I like the author's style; he tells it like it is, and he makes the information easy to digest. This is a very positive, powerful book that will help you get your life together. Definitely worth reading!"
~ Graciela Sholander

"Within a few pages I already had some simple ideas to easily implement into my life."
~ C. Wrightson

CONTENTS

To Chloe Sha,
For inspiring me to be more, do more and serve more.

Introduction

YOU ARE YOUR HABITS

If you're like most people, you probably harbor countless goals and aspirations: finally getting that promotion at work, eating a more balanced diet, saving money, losing weight, or being a more engaged parent. Prepared to make a major life change and with your sights set squarely on perfection, you fail—if not immediately, within the first few weeks.

Overwhelmed by the pressure of establishing several ambitious new habits at once, you throw your hands up in surrender, sit your two-year-old in front of *Frozen* for the third time this week, and break your three-day healthy eating streak as you sink your teeth into a double chocolate brownie.

Before you're too hard on yourself, though, take a moment to realize that this pattern is far more common than you may think. In fact, it's pretty safe to say that the majority of people setting lofty goals like eliminating debt, quitting smoking, or losing significant amounts of weight don't actually achieve them. **You are not the problem.**

To provide some evidence in case you aren't convinced, let's take a look at the success rate of New Year's resolutions in America. A study conducted by the University of Scranton found that only 8% of those who make New Year's resolutions on any given year actually achieve them. Interestingly, nearly one in four Americans who participate in setting New Year's resolutions have *never* successfully achieved them. While some may chalk it up to the many distractions of the indulgent American culture, I'd like to argue that similar results would be discovered in communities across the world.

The trouble with lofty goals like promotions, weight loss, and getting out of debt is that they often require major changes to our existing habits.

So why is it so difficult to introduce new habits into our daily routines?

Well, as it turns out, our modern-day understanding of the brain teaches us that large-scale behavioral changes are no easy feat. In fact, that 30-pound weight-loss goal you've just established for yourself may be setting you up to fail.

I know the path to personal transformation is starting to sound pretty hopeless, so here's the good news: *It doesn't have to be difficult.* The trick is having a sound strategy and manageable goals that won't drain all of your willpower. So instead of setting big, New Year's resolution-scale goals, **we're going to learn how to target keystone habits, and in just five to ten minutes a day, create major transformations in your life.**

That may sound like a big promise to make, but it's one that we'll keep. **By the end of this book, in addition to gaining a whole new understanding of habits, you'll be able to use them effectively to spark personal change.**

YOUR FREE GIFTS

As a thank-you for purchasing this book, I'd like to offer you these three bonus resources:

1. **Passcode to the *Discover Your Habit Roadmap* Quiz**
   How would you like to get personalized, individual feedback from our experts to help you achieve your goals? Take the quiz and we'll help you create a customized habits roadmap for FREE! Your results will also pinpoint specific tools in this book to help you achieve greater success in life and business.

2. **8 Steps to Defeating Any Limiting Label (PDF Guide)**
   Would you like to break through the limiting beliefs that are holding you back? Before you can make a shift in your external world, you need to make a shift in your internal world. This 8-step guide will help you do just that.

3. **Habit Case Study: How I Lost 15 Pounds of Fat in 3 Months**
   Would you like to use the power of habits to

transform your body? I've put together a case study that shows you how I used what I call the "five-minute habit" to get into the best shape of my life.

To get instant access, go here:
www.AkashKaria.com/Habits

ABOUT AKASH KARIA

Akash Karia is a peak performance coach who has trained over 120,000 people worldwide, from bankers in Hong Kong to senior executives in Thailand to government members in Dubai. He writes short, high-impact books on peak performance and psychology, and has twice been ranked as the **#1 Most Popular Business & Money Author** on Amazon Kindle.

"Akash is one of the best professional speakers in the world today...He has a great message, is motivating, inspiring and interactive at the same time...!"
~ Brian Tracy, CPAE Speaker Hall of Fame, #1 Bestselling Author of *Maximum Achievement*

"Akash is a phenomenal coach! The information I gained in just a few short hours is priceless."
~ Fatema Dewji, Director of Marketing for billion-dollar conglomerate, MeTL

"Akash delivered true value to our global sales team...relevant insights and tools that we can immediately implement in the market!"
~ Mark Butterman, Director, InFront Sports & Media AG

"Akash is THE best coach I've ever had!"
~ Eric Laughton, Certified John Maxwell Trainer

Subject to availability, Akash conducts keynotes, workshops and seminars internationally. Get in touch with him on www.AkashKaria.com/Keynotes (or via Akash@AkashKaria.com / akash.speaker@gmail.com).

Chapter 1

THE MAGIC OF SMALL HABITS

THE HIDDEN AGENCY OF HABITS

Before we dive into the nitty-gritty of "small habits" and how they can make your goals easier to achieve, it's important to understand the presence and sheer power of habits in our everyday lives.

Many of the things we do on a daily basis—stopping for coffee before work, reading the newspaper, taking a shower, exercising, watching TV, having a snack—are habits so programmed in our neurological pathways that we don't even know they exist. We move through our day like a plane on autopilot, automatically responding to the happenings of daily life based on the habits we've learned over time.

A short anecdote from the late American author David Foster Wallace illustrates this idea rather nicely. During his commencement speech at Kenyon

College, Wallace said:

> "There are these two young fish swimming along, and they happen to meet an older fish swimming the other way, who nods at them and says, 'Morning, boys, how's the water?' The two young fish swim on for a bit, and then eventually one of them looks over at the other and goes, 'What the hell is water?'"

"What's water?"

The idea is that even though the fish are surrounded by water every moment of their lives, they are unaware of its existence. The water is so much a part of their everyday reality that it goes unnoticed—or, as Wallace mentioned later in his speech, is "hidden in plain sight all around."

Human habits can be explained in much the same way. Although typically unseen and unnoticed by us, our habits are powerful enough to impact our decision-making and drive our daily activities. **In fact, Duke University researchers found that more than 40% "of our actions are unconscious habits."** This idea validates the saying "old habits die hard" and explains why new habits often are exceedingly difficult to establish.

So should you stop trying?

Absolutely not.

Your strategy for developing habits that actually stick, however, may need to change. Read on to learn how small habits can revolutionize your ability to achieve your goals gradually and painlessly by adjusting small behaviors.

SMALL HABITS DEFINED

We've discussed the link between goal setting, behavior change, and habits, and we've agreed that new habits involving significant changes to existing routines usually don't stick.

The logical solution?

Increase your chances of success by decreasing the scale of your undertaking. In other words, focus on establishing small habits instead.

Small habits, as the name implies, are those habits that are so small that they take very little willpower to carry out and thus make achieving them very likely.

BJ Fogg (www.tinyhabits.com), an experimental psychologist who teaches courses and directs the Persuasive Tech Lab at Stanford University, calls these habits "Tiny Habits"™ and says that the key to long-term change is to take baby steps. So, no matter what name you call them—"tiny habits" or "small habits"—the point is that by choosing to implement *small* behavioral changes, you can easily develop new habits with minimal effort.

So what are some examples of small habits you could perform on a daily basis to kick-start your personal transformation? Here's a quick list:

- Read for 10 minutes

- Do two push-ups
- Drink a small glass of water with lunch
- Stretch for one minute
- Write 25 words in your journal
- Put on your running shoes
- Sit down at piano
- Do one yoga pose
- Floss one tooth
- Laugh out loud once

The really great thing about these and other small habits—in addition to the fact that they're a cinch to establish in your daily routine—is that they have the potential to lead to larger-scale improvement. While doing one push-up per day may not seem like a huge accomplishment, it could very easily lead to doing two or three. Besides, one is better than none, right? And you're already standing in the bathroom holding a string of floss, so why not do a couple more teeth? Before you know it, you're flossing your teeth with all the skill and enthusiasm of a dental hygienist (Credit: BJ Fogg).

Do just one push-up

WHY SMALL HABITS WORK

So what is it about small habits that gives them some real staying power?

I'm glad you asked.

The many reasons they work can be easily summed up in three main points.

First and foremost, they require very little willpower. The importance of this point cannot be understated, because this is what separates small habits from the large, unwieldy ones. To illustrate this idea, let's break down the typical stages through which you progress when attempting to start a new habit.

Take the common goal to "become a runner," for example. After discovering that you need to be more active, you start planning. You could easily take some time after work every evening to go for a quick run, starting with two miles and gradually increasing your distance until you achieve your goal. You'll be a marathon runner in no time—complete with a trendy new athletic wardrobe and runner's physique.

It's day one, and things are off to a good start. You get home from work, lace up your new running shoes, turn on your new playlist, and head out the door. The first run goes well, as do the second and third. On day four, though, you stay a little later at work, and your legs are stiff. When you get home, you order some takeout, flip on the TV, and put your feet up. You don't really need to go for a run every night, right?

Before you know it, you've talked yourself out of running four nights in a row, and you're no longer feeling motivated and optimistic. Falling into a spiral of self-loathing, you ask yourself why you *never* manage to follow through.

It's pretty simple, really. If you cannot rally the amount of willpower necessary to achieve your new habit, you cannot succeed. Major new habits—like running every night, reading three books per month, or walking your dog every morning—require some major willpower.

The beauty of small habits is that they remove the willpower issue from the equation. Their small nature allows you to accomplish them using only minimal willpower. This prevents your brain from obsessing over how challenging your new habit is, and leaves you plenty of leftover willpower to build upon these habits and continue to introduce new ones.

The second reason small habits work so well is that they allow you to achieve "small wins." Rather than setting huge goals and failing, you can set multiple goals and experience success over and over. Researchers have found that when you achieve a small goal, you may actually experience a large sense of accomplishment that is disproportionate to the act itself.

You could compare this to the satisfaction of crossing small tasks off a long to-do list. No matter how small the task, it is often highly satisfying to cross it off the list and savor your small win. Your brain associates that sense of satisfaction with the completion of your task and motivates you to complete even more.

This transitions nicely into the third reason that the small habit strategy works so well: Small habits generate momentum. Think of it as a ripple effect. Fogg has drawn some insightful conclusions regarding how even small habits can lead to a shift in identity. He says:

> "You shift because of your own actions. But it's not just doing actions: It's YOU watching YOURSELF succeed, almost like you're someone else observing and drawing conclusions. I have a sense that's key. Seeing yourself perform new behaviors shifts your identity. And that creates ripple effects." - Via www.tinyhabits.com/sandbox

As you accomplish the small goals you set for yourself and form new small habits, your motivation snowballs as your own view of yourself changes. One day, you will wake up and realize that you're no longer the Lazy Person Who

Wants to Exercise But Can't. Instead, you're that Healthy, Active Coworker Who's Always Two Steps Ahead. The ability of small habits to unlock the human agency for change makes them a very powerful tool.

But the idea is to start small. Different people have varying levels of willpower, so take the time to learn how much you can handle. The small habit concept is as much about implementing new positive behaviors as it is about learning how well your own brain and body respond to change.

NOTE REGARDING THE BONUSES IN THIS BOOK

You'll notice that I'm including additional bonuses such as quizzes, MP3s, case studies and personalized feedback to go along with the book. These resources are designed to help take advantage of the different mediums and encourage you to take ACTION on the principles you learn.

None of these are resources essential to the book...but for those of you who want to continue your habits journey further than this book (free of charge, of course), then these resources are for you.

Chapter 2

THE REMARKABLE POWER
OF KEYSTONE HABITS

Now that you understand the concept of small habits, let's dive into another important concept in the world of behavior change research: keystone habits.

Charles Duhigg, award-winning New York Times reporter and author of the book *The Power of Habit: Why We Do What We Do in Life and Business*, has explored at length the idea of a "keystone habit," or a small change in routine that can set off a chain reaction of new and improved behaviors.

So what makes a keystone habit different from a small habit?

When you perform a small habit—say, for example, putting on your running shoes every morning—you are successful as soon as you put your running shoes on, whether or not you actually go for a run.

A keystone habit, on the other hand, is *only* a keystone habit if it eventually leads to other behavioral changes.

While small habits certainly have the potential to breed other habits, they are not by definition required to do so.

Additionally, a keystone habit, unlike a small habit, is not necessarily defined by its size. While a small habit could turn out to be a keystone habit (if, for example, a brief daily stretching routine leads to further exercise, healthy eating, and other positive new behaviors), a keystone habit does not have to be small. For instance, while taking a brisk stroll to the end of the driveway or around the yard is a bit too involved to be considered a small habit (as it involves putting on shoes, going outside, and actually accomplishing your walk), this daily routine could make a great keystone habit.

I say this because completing the task of walking to the end of the driveway and back is a small enough ritual to allow you to experience a small win each time. The success you experience will feel good, and you may very well build additional habits like spending more time outside, jogging around the block, and making other healthy decisions. Once established, keystone habits can act as a significant catalyst for change in your personal and professional life.

As this example illustrates, exercise is an example of one keystone habit that can have profound and far-reaching effects. There's no telling how the resulting improvements to confidence and energy levels could impact your personal and professional life; suddenly, you're waking up earlier to fit in your workout, making healthier food choices, and achieving higher levels of productivity at home and at work. The ability for even small amounts of exercise to affect your behavior in this way makes it a keystone habit well worth adopting.

To provide an example of a non-health-related keystone habit, experts in the field have found that the simple ritual of making your bed every morning can trigger additional behavior changes. Have you ever heard the old saying, "the state of your bed is the state of your head"? Based on our understanding of keystone habits, small wins, and willpower, there is actually some truth to this idea.

When you make your bed first thing in the morning, you're able to cross off the task and experience the satisfaction of a momentum-generating small win—all before you've had your coffee. Furthermore, research has actually linked the act of making your bed to other positive behaviors like improved productivity, happiness, and—according to Duhigg—even budgeting skills! As an added bonus, you've probably noticed that when you make your bed, the whole space seems tidier and more organized—even when the rest of the room is in disarray.

As an additional example, researchers have found that individuals who track their income and expenses on a regular basis are often more successful in other areas of their lives as well. So if you begin more closely tracking your expenses as a keystone habit, you'll begin discovering spending patterns that you may not have noticed before. This could lead you to be more cognizant of spending money when you shop, causing you to be make better decisions, spend your money more wisely, and ultimately increase your savings.

Tracking your income and expenses is a keystone habit

Once you experience these positive outcomes, you are likely to actually change the way you view yourself. Suddenly, once you are able to define yourself as a responsible person who plans for the future, you start making smarter decisions in other areas of your life as well.

In *The Power of Habit,* Duhigg includes a particularly interesting anecdote about how a simple keystone habit was able to make significant changes in a corporate workplace. In 1987, Paul O'Neill, the new CEO of Alcoa—or the Aluminum Company of America—was speaking to a large group of investors and stock analysts. To the crowd's dismay, rather than discussing profit margins and other business buzzwords, he wanted to discuss worker safety. Worker safety remained his primary focus, and it paid off. Duhigg recounts a conversation he had with O'Neill:

> "'I knew I had to transform Alcoa,' O'Neill told me, 'but you can't order people to change.

> "'That's not how the brain works. So I decided I was going to start by focusing on one thing. If I could start disrupting the habits around one thing, it would spread throughout the entire company.'"

In just one short year, the organization's profits reached a record high, and annual net income increased by 500%. Just the single keystone habit of focusing on worker safety caused a ripple effect throughout the company—also encouraging workers to recommend business improvements and much improving communication.

So three minutes per day spent making the bed could result in all these benefits? Absolutely. This is why we made the promise we did at the beginning of the book. By harnessing the power of even the smallest habits, you can transform your life in ways you never thought possible in just 10 minutes per day.

Chapter 3

THE 66-DAY CHALLENGE

So how long does it take to form a new habit?

This question often comes up as people prepare to implement new behaviors. The new action will inevitably be physically, emotionally, and/or mentally taxing, and it's natural to wonder how much time must pass before it becomes an automatic habit. If you've ever wondered about this yourself, you have most likely stumbled upon various books, articles, and blogs stating without any sort of scientific authority that any new habit can be formed in only 21 days!

If this sounds a little too good to be true, that's because it is.

So where did the legend of the 21-day habit formation come from?

This is actually an interesting story (courtesy of James Clear: www.jamesclear.com/new-habit). In the 1950s, a plastic surgeon named Maxwell Maltz began noticing that after operations, it took about 21 days for his patients to mentally adjust to their new images. For example, after a limb amputation, he found that it would typically take amputees 21 days to adjust to the loss and stop sensing a phantom limb.

He analyzed his own experiences with behavior change and ultimately published a book about this and some of his other theories in the 1960s, leading to the widespread conviction that habits only take 21 days to solidify. What Maltz actually said was, "These, and many other commonly observed phenomena tend to show that it requires a minimum of about 21 days for an old mental image to dissolve and a new one to jell."

The key word in this quotation—and the one that most tend to omit—is "minimum." The *minimum* amount of time it takes people to adjust to a new change or habit was observed by Maltz to be approximately 21 days. It stands to reason then that for many people, it could take much longer than 21 days for a new habit to become solidified. The most recent research on habit formation seems to support this concept as well.

Dr. Phillippa Lally, a psychologist at University College London, conducted a research study to determine how long the process of habit formation actually takes. During the study, which was accepted into the *European Journal of Social Psychology* in 2009, Lally and her colleagues followed the progress of 96 volunteers as they worked to form various habits. Based on information reported daily by participants, the study ultimately found that on average, it took 66 days for the participants' chosen behaviors to become automatic.

It is important to keep in mind, however, that the 66-day timeframe is an average and that depending on the person as well as the behavior chosen, the study found that the habit could take anywhere from 18 to 254 days to form. So rather than taking for granted that any new habit can be established within a set timeframe, understand that the time required to make a new habit stick can vary widely depending on the individual, the habit itself, and any other relevant circumstances impacting the habit's formation.

In another interesting development, the research article's abstract explains how Lally's team discovered that, "Missing one opportunity to perform the behavior did not materially affect the habit formation process." So even though it is important to be consistent and deliberate about establishing a new habit, perfection isn't a requirement.

Start your 66-day challenge today!

What can we learn from Lally's study on habit formation?

Well, while there's a chance your new habit could become automatic in as few as 21 days, there's an even bigger chance that it could take three months or more. Despite the time variation, however, having a timeframe to follow as you work toward achieving your goal can be very helpful.

Why?

Because telling yourself that you're going to make your bed every morning for the indefinite future sounds hard. Telling yourself you're going to make your bed every morning for 66 days sounds like a surmountable challenge. This second option allows you to chase the light at the end of the tunnel and send yourself the message that the hard part is temporary.

For this reason, using the 66-day average timeframe from Lally's research study as a guide, I encourage you to commit to the 66-day challenge. Apply the principles you learn throughout this book for the next 66 days to establish new, life-changing habits.

Chapter 4

WHAT'S YOUR KEYSTONE HABIT?

So you've done your research, and you have a pretty good understanding of how the habit formation process works. So what's next?

Baby steps. The next nine chapters will walk you through the process of actually implementing significant behavior change in your life. We will begin by identifying a keystone habit you would like to build into your life, but then break it down into small, achievable small habits.

Sounds easy enough, right?

In actuality, however, choosing a keystone habit can be one of the most challenging steps. **As you probably remember, a habit is a keystone only when it leads to other positive behavior change in your life.** So how are you supposed to know what specific habit will change, reprogram, and rearrange other behaviors that have become engrained into your daily routine?

For many people, a good keystone habit may revolve around ending an unhealthy behavior—like smoking, drinking, gambling, or negative thinking—and replacing it with a healthier routine.

For others, keystone habits are often healthy behaviors that are currently lacking, such as exercising, cooking healthy meals, reading more often, tracking expenses, or maintaining a journal or diary.

In case you're currently racking your brain for a suitable habit and coming up empty, consider choosing one from this list:

- Get more sleep
- Exercise regularly
- Wake up earlier
- Cook healthier meals
- Keep a gratitude journal
- Maintain a diary
- Record eating habits in a food journal
- Read on a regular basis
- Track your expenses
- Drink more water

- Make your bed
- Floss your teeth
- Meditate
- Establish a weekly cleaning routine

This is by no means an exhaustive list, but ask yourself whether any of them could lead to further positive behavior change in your life. For example, something as simple as maintaining a regular food journal can lead to healthier eating, more exercise, and increased productivity at work and at home.

So let's get started by choosing just one keystone habit you want to adopt—baby steps, remember?

IN A NUTSHELL:

- Step 1: Choose your ONE keystone habit. Write it down below:

_____

_____

_____

_____

_____

_____

_____

_____

_____

Free Bonus:
The 2-Page Habit Worksheet

Don't just read this book, take action! To help you, I've put together a two-page worksheet that you can download and use to immediately put these tools into practice. These two pages have the potential to transform your life. To get access, go here:
www.AkashKaria.com/Habits

Chapter 5

HOW SMALL HABITS HELP YOU GET STARTED

At some point in your life, you've probably heard someone use the phrase "start small." Maybe you were even the one imparting these words of wisdom. Now think back, and try to remember the surrounding circumstances—perhaps you or someone you know was preparing to make a significant change or take on a new challenge. The suggestion to start small is actually pretty well-founded advice and ultimately stems from the idea that adopting change gradually can help ease a challenging transition.

So once you've identified a keystone habit you wish to adopt, it's time to start small and break it down into a tinier, more manageable small habit. **For example, if your goal is to develop the keystone habit of exercising on a daily basis, begin simply by putting on your running shoes every morning.** The keystone habit you're hoping to develop is regular exercise, but the small habit that will make help to make that goal a reality is donning your favorite pair of running shoes.

Put on your running shoes every morning

Next, commit to performing your small habit every day for 66 days. As you gradually master the ability to lace up your shoes every day, don't be surprised if you find yourself stepping outside, walking up and down the driveway, taking a jog around the block, and even throwing in some push-ups.

Remember what we learned about small wins earlier? This is where small wins become really important because they allow you to experience easy successes on a daily basis, and your brain likes success. It's addicting. **Every time you perform your small habit, you win, and you come one step closer to developing a keystone habit that will stick around for the long haul.**

To help these small wins really sink in and cement a new sticky habit, it is important to be consistent. If you are not performing your small habit on a daily basis, your brain won't detect the new routine, and it is then much harder for the action to become automatic. While absolute perfection isn't required, and it's okay to skip a day here and there for good reason, daily adherence to your new routine will go a long way in forming a successful new habit.

Since a good small habit is typically one that requires very little willpower, you may find that you actually master it in no time at all! If that's the case, feel free to incorporate some additional small habits into your daily routine. For instance, actions as simple as performing one stretch before bed, drinking a glass of water after lunch, or making your bed when you wake up in the morning could also contribute to your overall goal of adopting a daily exercise regimen.

BIG-PICTURE THINKING

Even though small habits aren't very taxing, 66 days can feel like a long time. If you tire of your small habit or begin trying to talk yourself out if it on certain days, you're probably in good company because habit formation isn't always easy. Even the tiniest of habits require a small change to your routine, and your brain is programmed to resist those changes.

What can you do to improve your chances of success even further?

The answer is simple: focus on the big picture. In this case, the big picture is the keystone habit you selected back in Chapter 4. Take a look at the example below to understand how the goal, the small habit, and big-picture thinking can work in your best interest.

Keystone habit goal:
Cook healthy meals on a daily basis

Small habits:
Put a pot on the stove
Eat one serving of fruit and/or vegetables
Find one simple, nutritious recipe

Big-Picture Thinking:

I want to become a healthier person who can prepare and cook nutritious, well-balanced meals on a regular basis.

Although your day-to-day activities revolve around executing your chosen small habits, your focus should remain on your big-picture keystone habit goal. Rather than dwelling on any inconvenience involved in performing your small habits, dwell on the overall outcome you are hoping to achieve. Say it out loud if you have to, because this big-picture thinking can be a strong motivational tool to have in your toolbox.

There's actually some science behind big-picture thinking. During a study that focused on the factors influencing self-control, Dr. Kentaro Fujita and his colleagues at Ohio State University (http://bit.ly/Fujita-Research) discovered through a number of experiments that individuals who were thinking in an abstract, or high-level way exhibited greater self-control than those thinking in a concrete, or low-level way.

You could compare this difference in perspective to the difference between seeing all the stars in the sky and focusing on just a single star. **The participants who were asked to focus on big-picture concepts (i.e., *why* they exercise as opposed to *how*) were ultimately more successful in exhibiting self-control under various circumstances.**

So to improve your self-control and increase your chances of successfully adopting your keystone habit, keep your thoughts centered on your goal.

Start small, but dream big.

IN A NUTSHELL:

- Step 1: Choose your keystone habit
- Step 2: Create a small habit (write it down below):

_____

_____

_____

_____

_____

_____

_____

_____

_____

Chapter 6

LET'S BRING IN FREUD...

According to Freudian psychology (http://bit.ly/pain-pleasure), human beings are innately motivated by the constant push and pull of pleasure and pain. We chase after things that will bring us either biological or psychological pleasure, and we avoid things that cause pain. This concept has been coined the "pain-pleasure principle" and has been acknowledged by ancient and modern thought leaders alike.

"We may lay it down that Pleasure is a movement, a movement by which the soul as a whole is consciously brought into its normal state of being; and that Pain is the opposite."
— Aristotle

"Nature has placed mankind under the governance of two sovereign masters, pain, *and* pleasure."
— Jeremy Bentham

"The secret of success is learning how to use pain and pleasure instead of having pain and pleasure use you. If you do that, you're in control of your life. If you don't, life controls you."
— Anthony Robbins

So how does the pain-pleasure principle apply to the habit-creation process?

Let me explain by asking you a few questions.

Why did you fail to achieve your New Year's resolution to go to the gym four times a week?

Because your brain associates it with pain, and as we just learned, the brain is wired to avoid pain under most circumstances.

Why do you binge-watch *Orange Is the New Black* every evening until you go to bed instead of getting your work done?

Watching TV brings you pleasure, while your brain associates work with pain. Not only would you have to turn off the TV (a painful task in and of itself), but you would have to buckle down and be productive.

So if you've been experiencing some resistance in your attempts to build a new habit, one very likely reason is that you are associating the action with some sort of physical or psychological pain. As a result—although your new habit could improve your life—you avoid it like the plague.

The logical solution here is to flip that mental association from a painful one to a pleasant one by using a reward system. The reward you choose will help motivate you to execute your habit and increase the likelihood that you will continue to carry it out.

Dan Ariely, a professor of psychology at Duke University, put the pain-pleasure principle into practice when he was unfortunately infected with hepatitis C. To cure himself, he was instructed to inject himself three days per week with interferon. Lasting for 18 months and resulting in some severe side effects such as fever, vomiting, and dizziness, this particular treatment regimen isn't exactly easy to stick to.

So what did Ariely do? According to his best-selling book, *Predictably Irrational,* he used a reward system to help make his medication schedule more manageable.

On the days he had to administer an injection, he would reward himself with watching one of his favorite movies. Because he was a movie lover, this strategy helped him to alter his mental associations with injection.

Impressively, after he followed through with his treatment for the required 18 months, Ariely's doctors told him that he was actually the *only* one of their patients who had been able to take the medication regularly. The other patients were understandably unable to overcome the pain associated with taking the medicine regularly as prescribed.

So how can you use this principle to help make your habit easier to achieve?

Develop a simple rewards system that will help change the negative associations you have with the habit to positive ones. Here are some strategies you can use to help associate your habits with pleasure rather than pain.

1 – MAKE IT FUN
Habits like exercising, cooking healthy meals, or reading more are often difficult to stick with because

they aren't necessarily enjoyable for everyone. Exercising is exhausting and often boring, and cooking healthy meals is nowhere near as fun as eating out on a regular basis. So, rather than struggling through activities you don't enjoy for a couple of weeks before dropping them altogether, look for ways to make them fun.

For example, if the habit you're hoping to establish is going for a run on a daily basis, create a playlist you love, and find a buddy to go with you. If good music and good company help you to associate running with a more pleasurable experience, you will be far more likely to follow through.

2 – CHOOSE A REWARD

As obvious as this sounds, choose as a reward something that you really love. It is essential to the success of the reward system that the pleasure of receiving the reward outweighs the pain associated with carrying out the habit. If the reward isn't good enough, it will be too easy to talk yourself out of it.

3 – VISUALIZE THE REWARD

Get excited about your reward by imagining the moment you get to enjoy it. Imagine how much pleasure your reward will bring you to help outweigh the pain associated with completing the habit itself.

4 – ASSOCIATE REWARD WITH HABIT

Once you've imagined the pleasure your reward will bring you, associate that pleasure with the completion of the habit. Remind yourself that you can enjoy your reward only if you carry out your habit.

5 – ENJOY YOUR REWARD

As soon as you successfully carry out your habit, follow through with your reward.

6 – PENALIZE FAILURE

For many people, the hardest part of having a successful reward system is having the discipline to withhold the reward when you fail to execute your habit. For example, if your reward for successfully completing a morning workout is purchasing a cup of coffee from Starbucks before work, it can be extremely challenging to drive past Starbucks without stopping when you fail to actually complete your workout. **However, you must make a committed DECISION that you will not allow yourself to enjoy your reward because you failed to complete your workout.** As simple as it sounds, consciously making a committed decision will make it likely that you will follow through.

Additionally, if you do fail to carry out your habit, it is important to spend some time trying to examine why the failure occurred. If there's a possibility that the pull of the reward isn't strong enough, consider using a more powerful reward to ensure you'll push through any pain associated with the completion of your habit.

So as you're gearing up to add a new habit to your daily routine, tap into the human instinct to avoid pain and pursue pleasure by rewarding yourself for your success.

After all, you deserve it!

IN A NUTSHELL:

- Step 1: Choose your keystone habit
- Step 2: Create a small habit
- Step 3: Choose your reward.

What's your reward? Don't just read! Write it down in your worksheet (www.AkashKaria.com/Habits) or diary:

_____

_____

_____

_____

_____

_____

_____

_____

_____

Chapter 7

MY FAVORITE TECHNIQUE FOR BUILDING HABITS

Part of the challenge involved in establishing a new habit—especially at the very beginning—is simply remembering to carry it out.

Despite your best intentions, your new flossing habit will inevitably fall by the wayside as soon as you find yourself running late for work and dashing out of the house without so much as a backward glance at the trail of frenzied kitchen destruction you left in your wake.

To help make your habit a more automatic part of your daily routine, **various experts have found that it is often helpful to use an external cue or trigger that acts as a reminder that it's time to execute your habit.** Ideally, the cue will be something that you are already consistently doing or interacting with on a daily basis. If the cue has already been hard-wired into your daily routine, and you always execute your habit immediately after the cue, your habit is that much more likely to become similarly engrained.

So how can you identify a good cue?

First, identify some activities you do every day in the same way and/or around the same time. For instance, perhaps every morning after your shower, you hang your towel on the hook behind the door. Because that's a relatively consistent activity, you could use that as a cue to trigger your habit. **If your goal is to do three push-ups every day, you could do them as soon as you hang your towel up on the hook.**

Or maybe you put your slippers on every morning when you get out bed. That's the perfect time to make your bed, do some stretching, or spend 15 minutes writing in a journal. Because whichever new habit you choose, you are far more likely to continue on with the rest of your plan to engage in your new habit if it is linked specifically to the daily action of sliding on your slippers.

This whole concept of taking advantage of your existing daily routine to anchor new habits is what Peter Gollwitzer, a professor of psychology at New York University and leading researcher on the psychology behind goal-setting and planning, refers to as "if-then" planning or "implementation intentions." There have actually been quite a few studies that ultimately discovered people are truly more successful in accomplishing their goals when they plan their intentions in advance.

For example in one study (www.bit.ly/procrastination-study), German participants were asked whether they would voluntarily commit to writing and submitting an essay about their experiences on Christmas Eve by December 26. Half of the participants were also asked about when, where, and how they would be writing their essays.

Those who engaged in if-then planning were actually three times more likely to successfully complete the essay. **The results speak for themselves: 71% of the participants who established implementation intentions actually followed through with the task, while only 32% of the participants in the other group sent in their essays.**

What's your if-then plan?

Another research study focused on participants who were attempting to establish a regular exercise routine. **Of those who used an if-then planning strategy to help stick to their goal, 91% were successful in following through. In comparison, only 39% of the participants who did not use if-then planning were able to stick to their exercise routine.** These two studies are not alone. In fact, there have been somewhere in the ballpark of 100 other studies conducted that similarly prove the power of if-then planning.

So what's the takeaway for those of us trying to develop some new sticky habits?

You can think of it like this:

If you've just finished putting your kids to bed, **then** you wash any dishes piled in the sink.

If it's 2 p.m., **then** you will spend 30 minutes returning calls.

If you change your clothes after coming home from work, **then** you turn on your Jillian Michaels workout DVD.

If you finish your cup of coffee at work, **then** you pour yourself a glass of water.

If it's 6 p.m., **then** you throw on your gym clothes and go for a run.

You get the picture: Existing environmental cue plus new habit equals an improved chance of success. You may have also noticed that each of the sample goals or habits mentioned above is positive, or an action that you *will* be taking as soon as you encounter the designated cue. When you're developing your if-then strategies, you'll want to avoid doing the opposite by setting negative goals, or goals in which your plan is *not* to do something.

Here are a few examples:

> If I become stressed out at work, then I'm **not** going to grind my teeth.

> If I get bored, then I'm **not** going to eat a snack.

> If I'm hungry, then I'm **not** going to each chocolate.

> If it's Saturday morning, then I'm **not** going to sleep in past 8.

> If I get frustrated with my kids, then I'm **not** going to yell.

Why are negative if-then goals problematic?

They actually focus your attention on the action you are hoping to avoid. Rather than reprogramming yourself to focus on performing a new habit in place of a bad one, you're actually allowing your brain to linger on the bad habit. This increased awareness of the action you're not supposed to be doing can make it significantly harder for you to succeed.

So focus on the positive, and take some time to plan when, where, and how you're going to accomplish your goal. Not only does this approach allow you to increase your odds of success by linking the new habit to an existing one, but it also helps automate and expedite the decision-making process.

How?

Well, you effectively eliminate the need to consciously make the decision later by hardwiring your brain to act a certain way upon encountering a specific future scenario. For example, rather than coming home and agonizing over whether or not you should go for a run before dinner, you will have already done the hard part by deciding in advance that as soon as you change out of your work clothes, you will go for a run.

Now don't expect this to be easy right away. Picking up a new habit, as you have surely already learned at some point in your life, takes dedication and patience. The concept of if-then planning, much like the other strategies discussed in this book, can help you increase your chances of success and become more in tune with your habit formation strengths and weaknesses.

IN A NUTSHELL:

- Step 1: Choose your keystone habit
- Step 2: Create a small habit
- Step 3: Choose your reward
- Step 4: Use an "if-then" strategy.

Write down an if-then goal below:

_____

_____

_____

_____

_____

_____

_____

_____

_____

Free Bonus:
Companion Course: 9 Steps to Elite Performance

I talk about the "if-then" strategy in more depth in my video course, "9 Steps for Elite Performance." This video course reveals the mindset hacks you can use to create new habits and achieve your goals. It currently retails for $20, but you can grab it for free as my gift to you: www.AkashKaria.com/Habits

Chapter 8

THE REALIST AND THE OPTIMIST WENT TO A BAR...

"All you have to do is believe in yourself."

"Reach for the stars!"

"If you believe it, you can achieve it."

"Dream big!"

You've probably heard these phrases—or variations of them—many times before because in this day and age, we are enamored by the idea of endless possibility and the inner strength of the individual. Being a "glass half full" type of person myself, I also tend to believe that a little bit of optimism can go a long way when it comes to habit formation.

But it's not just me—many studies over the years have found that people who maintain a more positive, optimistic outlook tend to have healthier lives and relationships. Additionally, numerous studies related to optimism have focused on success in the business world specifically. **For example, one study (www.bit.ly/optimism-study) that focused on the performance of sales personnel at one organization found that those who scored high on an optimism test upon joining the sales team actually sold 37% more product in their first two years than their coworkers.**

Optimism has also been found to be an especially important trait for entrepreneurs; those with a positive outlook enjoy their work more and have an easier time convincing others of their ability to achieve the impossible. You can probably think of a few people like this. They are often effective in not only leading others, but inspiring them to strive for higher levels of performance and innovation.

But before you skip off to watch *Pollyanna* and make a list of 36 habits you're going to implement starting tomorrow (because all you have to do is believe, right?), **it's important to understand that optimism without realism can actually do you more harm than good.** The problem with optimism is that it often fails to recognize potential challenges and **actually tricks your mind into feeling like**

you've accomplished your goal before you even start.

Optimism without realism tricks your mind into celebrating a victory you haven't even accomplished yet.

As a result, you are likely to put forth much less effort and subsequently run out of steam long before your habit becomes automatic. Gabriele Oettingen, a psychology professor at both New York University and the University of Hamburg, has conducted some studies that clearly illustrate this idea. In a 2014 New York Times article, Oettingen described one such study as follows:

> "In a 2011 study published in the Journal of Experimental Social Psychology, we asked

two groups of college students to write about what lay in store for the coming week. One group was asked to imagine that the week would be great. The other group was just asked to write down any thoughts about the week that came to mind. The students who had positively fantasized reported feeling less energized than those in the control group. As we later documented, they also went on to accomplish less during that week." – Via www.bit.ly/nyt-study

So why did the group that was asked to practice positive thinking achieve less? Oettingen explains, **"Positive thinking fools our minds into perceiving that we've already attained our goal, slackening our readiness to pursue it."**

If optimism alone isn't the answer, then what kind of mindset is best for setting and achieving your goals?

This is where realistic optimism, or the ability to think positively about the future while still recognizing any barriers that may stand in your way, comes in. Oettingen and her colleagues refer to this process as "mental contrasting." She explains, "When participants have performed mental contrasting with reasonable, potentially attainable wishes, they have come away more energized and achieved better results compared with participants who either positively fantasized or dwelt on the obstacles."

Use mental contrasting to be more successful.

In another study focused on exercise and healthy eating, Oettingen found that the participants who had spent time performing a "planning exercise" to help them overcome any obstacles were exercising twice as long and "eating considerably more vegetables" four months later.

So what's our sticky habit takeaway here?
Be optimistic, but be realistic as well.

It's a delicate balance, but it's one that needs to be made. **Realistic optimists have the ability to consciously acknowledge the challenges they may encounter in establishing their new habit and start making plans to overcome them.** Unrealistic optimists fail to acknowledge the fact that there will be challenges, so when challenges arise, they are unprepared. Their blind optimism sets them up for failure because they soon realize that the journey to losing 45 pounds isn't an easy one, and the process of quitting smoking isn't a glamorous one.

Once the excitement of committing to a positive change wears off, you are inevitably faced with the reality that the work ahead of you won't be easy. If you aren't ready for that reality, it could be enough to make you throw in the towel and walk away.

Is all of this starting to sound a little too familiar?

If it is, you're not alone, and you've come to the right place. As we have discussed time and again throughout this book, *the process of creating habits that actually stick is not easy*. It's simple, but it's not easy.

Hopefully the optimist in you wasn't gleefully skimming over those parts, because this knowledge is ultimately going to help you succeed. It doesn't mean you have to abandon your happy-go-lucky optimistic tendencies and trade them in for a permanent raincloud of pessimism. That wouldn't be productive either.

We're not looking to crush your dreams entirely, after all—we just want to balance them with a healthy dose of reality.

So what will this balance look like as you're preparing to execute your new habits? Follow these steps to help adopt a "realistic optimist" outlook:

1. **Visualize success.** The scientists have spoken: Optimism is good! Let yourself indulge in spending a few glorious moments visualizing yourself successfully completing your small habits and adopting your new behavior. Don't dwell on this for too long, though, before moving on to the next step.

2. **Imagine the obstacles.** Think about the habits you're planning to implement, and visualize the challenges you're sure to encounter. For example, if you are hoping to exercise on a daily basis, what obstacles could

get in your way? Well, you could oversleep, become sore or injured, or simply struggle to find the motivation to get up and go. Maybe your friends or family want to get together when you really should be heading to the gym. Ask yourself what kind of things are likely to keep you from performing your habit as planned.

3. **Identify a few solutions.** Once you've imagined a few of the challenges you might have to face, put a little time into thinking about how you would respond to each scenario. This doesn't have to be extremely detailed, and you certainly don't have to have all the answers. The important part is that you've recognized the fact that you will face obstacles, and you've got a couple workarounds up your sleeve.

So just for fun, let's revise some of those inspirational phrases listed at the beginning of the chapter.

> "All you have to do is believe in yourself and engage in some mental contrasting."

"Reach for the stars! (But don't forget to pack a parachute.)"

"If you believe it and acknowledge the challenges you are sure to encounter, you can achieve it!"

"Dream big, but always have a back-up plan!"

The revised versions may not make for great bumper stickers or graduation cards, but the idea behind them is infinitely more valuable.

If you can learn to split the difference between optimism and pessimism and approach life as a realistic optimist, you can enjoy the best of both worlds: positivity and hope in the face of challenge, and the resilience you need to be successful.

IN A NUTSHELL:

- Step 1: Choose your keystone habit
- Step 2: Create a small habit
- Step 3: Choose your reward
- Step 4: Use an "if-then" strategy
- Step 5: Be a realistic-optimist

What are some of the obstacles / temptations you will face when pursuing to create your new habit? Don't underestimate any obstacles – be realistic about the difficulty they will post for you:

_____

_____

_____

_____

_____

_____

_____

_____

_____

Chapter 9

GOT FRIENDS?

Have you found that it's easier to complete undesirable, mundane, or challenging tasks when you're with a friend? When I shared this principle with one of my friends, she recounted this story:

> "I can remember learning this concept as early as sixth grade when my dad asked me to rake the leaves in the yard. I stood in the backyard with the rake in my hand looking around dejectedly at the endless piles of leaves and pine needles. As I was halfheartedly pushing leaves around the yard and daydreaming about riding my new bicycle, a friend of mine wandered into the yard from the house next door.
>
> "Not willing to release me from my responsibility or send my friend home, my dad handed him a rake with a high-five and a smile. We had that yard raked in no time at all, and it was *fun!* Before we knew it, we were

busily engaged in a contest to create the biggest leaf pile in the yard. Then, once the yard was cleaned up, we were able to play a long game of catch in the crisp autumn air."

When you're working towards a common goal with a friend as a partner, the work becomes something fun you want to do because you're in the company of someone you like. This is common for students in high school and college especially. Studying is far more enjoyable when you can turn it into a group event. Even exercising can be fun when you're hitting the gym with a friend.

Most importantly, however, these people hold you accountable. If you and your friend make a regular plan to exercise, it is significantly harder to give up because your decision to skip a day will affect your friend, too. Additionally, your friend can help hold you accountable by knocking on your door, calling you, or texting you when it's time to go.

CHOOSING AN ACCOUNTABILITY PARTNER

To make your habits easier to accomplish, consider choosing an accountability partner to help motivate you and combat your excuses. You'll want to be selective when making your decision, however, because this person will play an important role in your habit formation process.

So how do you pick out an accountability partner?

Try choosing someone who has characteristics and behavioral patterns that you wish to emulate. You'll likely be spending a significant amount of time with this person, so it's important that your partner will be a positive influence on your daily routine. For example, if you're attempting to cook a healthy meal at home four nights a week, don't pick your friend who eats nothing but takeout as your accountability partner. It'll be much easier to talk yourself out of putting in the effort to grocery shop and cook if your friend is just going to make a quick stop at the local Chinese restaurant.

Don't underestimate the power of this principle. It sounds clichéd, but it's true: Friends can make / break your habits.

Similarly, a friend who has been exercising on a regular basis for years is a better choice than one who sporadically goes for a run every couple of months. When you're trying to establish a new exercise habit, it's important to have the perspective of someone who understands the importance of being consistent and can help motivate you when you're not feeling up to it.

Next, you'll want to make sure the person you choose is willing to show you some good old-fashioned tough love. The last thing you need when you've skipped a day of your habit is someone telling you that it's really not that big of a deal and sympathizing with each and every one of your excuses. Quite the opposite actually: You need someone who can shoot down your excuses and motivate you to follow through (but also encourage you and be loving / supportive when needed).

It's important, however, that you communicate clearly with this person about when you'll need to be pushed and when you just need some support and encouragement. This will help ensure you don't get burned out and frustrated with your accountability partner.

JOIN A GROUP

Your accountability partner doesn't necessarily have to be one single person. In fact, a group of people who share your interests or goals can be just as powerful in motivating you to achieve your objective.

Weight Watchers is a well-known example of a popular, successful accountability group that focuses on supporting people who want to lose weight by not only educating them about healthy eating options, but offering support in the form of both online and local accountability groups. Individuals who have joined this program can meet other people who are also working hard to lose weight and establish healthy eating habits. When a member of the group is struggling, the others can offer helpful advice and words of encouragement.

As another example, for those hoping to develop more consistent reading or writing habits, book clubs and writers' groups can be an invaluable resource. A book club offers both a fun social experience and a little bit of healthy peer pressure to read each assigned novel. Writers' groups are helpful in holding writers accountable to accomplish their writing goals through online and in-person forums. Members of an online group can post their own work online for review, constructively critique the writing of others, and discuss a variety of writing-related topics with peers.

Other accountability groups include the likes of Alcoholics Anonymous (AA), study groups, or any other group that helps motivate individuals with similar interests to accomplish their goals. When you surround yourself with a group of like-minded people, the work you're doing becomes more enjoyable, and you get the added bonus of having a whole group cheering you on and holding you accountable to your goal.

WRITE IT DOWN

Another strategy that could improve your chances of success is taking the time to write down your goals—or in this case, the new habits you've decided to implement in your everyday life. **A study conducted at Dominican University** (http://bit.ly/goals-research)**actually found that people who put their goals in writing were able to achieve about 50% more than their peers with non-written goals.** The study also found that participants who wrote down their goals were even more successful when they publicly broke down their goals into further "actionable commitments" and were held accountable by a friend via weekly progress reports.

Stop! And go write down your goal if you haven't already

Is the prospect of producing a weekly progress report sounding a little intimidating? Or time-consuming? Or like even more paperwork that you'll have to grudgingly deal with on a weekly basis?

That's okay. You don't have to write up a page-long summary of your successes and failures for the week to make this work (although if that sounds like fun to you, by all means go for it!). Instead, combine your written goals with public accountability in a way that jibes with your lifestyle. Blog it, Tweet it, Instagram it, put it on Facebook, text it to your kids, rant about it on your podcast—whatever works for you!

Let's take Facebook, for example. If you post a status on Facebook about how you're going to head to the gym after work for spinning class, it's likely that a couple of friends or family members will "like" your status. This informs you that they're aware of your plans and might even ask you about how your spinning class went the next time they see you. You wouldn't want to have to say, "Well, I was too lazy to go after work, so I went home, sat on the couch, and ate an entire carton of Rocky Road instead." So when the fatigue hits you on your way home and you just want to skip your workout, you go—because you already told your friends you were going.

I do what I teach. Here's me posting about my intention to go to the gym the next day for Muay Thai (martial arts) training:

Then, once you've successfully completed your goal for the day, don't be afraid to share that, too!

As you share your progress, the encouragement you receive from your friends and family will go a long way in helping you continue down your sticky habit path. (Of course, there will be some haters. But, like Taylor Swift says, "the haters gonna hate").

Using this strategy, I've checked in 148 workouts so far this year.

And that's helped me go from looking like this:

To this:

I'm not saying that you HAVE to publicly share your goals to achieve results. That works for me. But perhaps you prefer to keep your goals and your progress private. The point simply is that you should write down your goals (whether that's publicly or privately).

PICKING A CONSEQUENCE/PAIN

To aid in holding yourself accountable to your accountability partner (whoever or whatever that may be), establish a consequence for failing to complete your habit. For example, tell your spouse that every day you fail to execute your habit of reading for at least 30 minutes, you'll pay him or her $10. You could even up the ante by increasing this amount for every additional consecutive day that you skip.

The consequence doesn't necessarily have to be monetary. Instead of giving your friend, spouse, or coworker money when you skip your habit, maybe you'll offer to wash the dishes, make extra cold calls, or weed the garden. Whatever the consequence, it's important that you follow through. If you tell your spouse that you'll mow the lawn if you don't floss your teeth every night before bed, you can't take it back when you actually do miss a flossing session.

With this in mind, make sure you choose consequences that you will actually carry out should the need arise. Because follow-through is important when using this consequence strategy, it is probably wise to refrain from slapping a consequence with every habit you're hoping to establish. Instead, choose just one habit that might require a little extra motivation to keep you on track.

IN A NUTSHELL:

- Step 1: Choose your keystone habit
- Step 2: Create a small habit
- Step 3: Choose your reward
- Step 4: Use an "if-then" strategy
- Step 5: Be a realistic-optimist
- Step 6: Recruit an accountability partner.

Write down the name of your accountability partner / group:

_____

_____

_____

_____

_____

_____

_____

_____

_____

Free Bonus:
Case Study: How I Transformed My Body

Would you like to use the power of small habits to transform your body? I've put together a case study that shows you how I used the "five-minute habit" to get into the best shape of my life. Download it here: www.AkashKaria.com/Habits

Chapter 10

SHAPE YOUR ENVIRONMENT

If you were to follow every single step in this book, it would still be difficult to succeed without also following this one. If your environment is not structured in a way that will support the habits you're attempting to develop, it will be exponentially harder to follow through consistently. One of my friends explained this principle in this way:

> "Think of it like trying to grow a lemon tree. Most varieties of lemon trees thrive in warm, tropical climates (think California, Florida, Hawaii, Puerto Rico, etc.) and will ideally also be protected from strong wind. So if you live in the Midwest, a lemon tree in your backyard probably won't survive for long—even if you visualize a full-grown lemon tree and follow the proper protocol for planting a lemon tree. Despite your best efforts, the freezing temperatures, strong winds, and other extreme weather conditions common to the

typical Midwest climate will be too much for your lemon tree to handle.

"Developing a new habit in an environment that isn't supportive can be just as difficult as growing a lemon tree in the Midwest."

So what kinds of environments can be harmful to habit formation?

Well, this can really depend on the habit as well as your own personality or preferences. For example, if you're making a commitment to write on a daily basis, it's important to make sure that you have daily access to an environment with minimum distractions that will help you focus and encourage creativity. This might mean having a quiet office with a beautiful view in your own home, or maybe it would mean walking over to the local café.

As a writer myself, I've found over time that I'm able to be more productive at a café near my home. If I'm having trouble getting motivated to write, I'll head over to the café, and my work is instantly more enjoyable. For whatever reason, I find the quiet hum of voices in the background and the smell of coffee comforting and pleasant, which is important when I'm settling in to do some serious writing.

So how can you create an environment that works for you and your habit? Here are some tips and considerations that may help you discover an ideal setting for your developing habits.

1. CHOOSE AN ENVIRONMENT THAT YOU ENJOY

Like my example above about writing in a café, an environment that you find to be enjoyable can be an invaluable tool for solidifying a new habit. So if you're struggling to cement a new habit in your daily routine, consider changing something about your current environment to make it more enjoyable to you.

For example, if going to the gym to run on a treadmill everyday bores you to death, you could consider running somewhere a little more interesting. If you live close to a city, maybe you'd have more fun running through an urban environment where lots of other people are out and about. Or maybe you'd rather run through a quiet neighborhood, through a park, or near a large body of water. Weather permitting, find a place that you truly like to be, and run there instead.

What enjoyable environments can help encourage your desired behavior?

What if you're trying to develop a habit like cooking healthy meals that you can't physically move to a more enjoyable location?

Make changes to your existing environment to make it more fun. For example, if cooking healthy meals is your habit, maybe pouring yourself a glass of wine and turning on your favorite music will transform cooking into an event that you look forward to. Rather than having to dread standing around in your kitchen for an hour while you prep and cook your

food, you may even anticipate that "me time" you get
to have at the end of each day.

2. ELIMINATE DISTRACTIONS

New habits all over the world are thwarted on a daily
basis by temptations and distractions like junk food,
cigarettes, television, children, pets, unfolded laundry,
Facebook, text messages, and more. So eliminate
known distractions from your environment before
they interrupt your new habit and keep you from
reaching your goals consistently.

Are you constantly interrupted in the middle of your
yoga practice by your kids? You may want to
consider moving this activity to a time when the kids
are either at school or in bed for the night. Are you
unable to sit down and record your finances because
other unfinished chores like laundry and dishes
demand your attention? Make an effort to finish
these types of household chores ahead of time so
your attention isn't pulled away.

Is your daily reading routine regularly interrupted by
text messages from your friend? Or worse yet, when
you fall asleep? Answer any text messages, return any
urgent calls, and put your phone on silent in another

room before cracking open your book. If falling asleep while reading is a frequent problem for you, consider reading at a different time of day. Instead of making it the last thing you do before you go to sleep at night, wake up a little earlier in the morning, read during your lunch hour, or do your reading right after dinner.

So as you're working on implementing new habits, pay close attention to the factors that motivate or distract you. Every time you fail to carry out your habit, take some time to figure out why so that you can work on perfecting your routine.

3. PREPARE EVERYTHING IN ADVANCE

The last thing you want to do when trying to develop a new behavior is create unnecessary work for yourself. For example, if you've decided you're going to go for a jog every morning, don't wait until the morning to gather everything you'll need. If your iPod is in the kitchen, your gym shoes are in the front hall closet, and your favorite gym shorts are in a laundry basket in the basement, you're far less likely to get out of bed in the morning to get to the gym. That's a lot of work to get done first thing in the morning—especially when you'll still need to pack your bag and fill up a water bottle.

Increase your chance of success by packing your bag and gathering everything else you'll need the night before. When your alarm goes off in the morning, all you'll have to do is roll out of bed, change your clothes, grab your gym bag, and go.

You could apply this same concept to cooking, too. For instance, if you're planning on cooking a meal after work, it's pretty easy to talk yourself out of it if you still need to go grocery shopping, thaw the meat, gather all the ingredients, and do all the prep work. A little bit of planning in advance can significantly reduce the amount of work you'll have to do when you're actually ready to cook.

As an example, planning your meals for the week in advance allows you to make a grocery list and go shopping on the weekend. Then you'll know which meal you're planning to make each evening so that you can thaw any meat you might need and set out any dry ingredients the night before. When you get home in the evening, you'll be ready with everything you need to get right to work and cook a healthy meal.

The ability to mold your environment to fit your needs is invaluable as you work to implement and nurture new habits. So study your personal preferences and tendencies, and learn to take control of your surroundings.

IN A NUTSHELL:

- Step 1: Choose your keystone habit
- Step 2: Create a small habit
- Step 3: Choose your reward
- Step 4: Use an "if-then" strategy
- Step 5: Be a realistic-optimist
- Step 6: Recruit an accountability partner
- Step 7: Shape your environment to encourage the behavior

Chapter 11

THE SEINFELD WAY OF BUILDING HABITS

Between 2005 and 2007, the world-famous Spanish professional tennis player Rafael Nadal won 81 consecutive games on a clay court surface. In the sports world, winning streaks inspire excitement and headlines as fans and opponents alike cheer on teams and competitors who are performing well consistently.

A sign in a warehouse that reads, "This department has worked 146 days without an injury" inspires a high level of motivation to continue the streak. As the streak grows, so too does the corresponding level of disappointment when the streak is broken.

As these examples illustrate, winning streaks are not only impressive accomplishments, but powerful motivators. **You can apply this concept to your sticky habit creation process by going on a "winning streak" or creating a chain of success.**

For this step, it's important that your chain of success is something visual, because seeing your winning streak on a daily basis will motivate you to keep it going.

So what kind of visual tool should you use to help hold yourself accountable?

One of my favorite visuals for the success chain is the Jerry Seinfeld calendar. A successful American comedian, he is probably most well-known for his sitcom *Seinfeld*. As a comedian, it was important for him to be writing on a daily basis. So to help motivate himself, he hung a large wall calendar and placed a big red "X" on every day that he did some writing with the goal of creating a long chain of X's. According to Seinfeld, **"You'll like seeing that chain, especially when you get a few weeks under your belt. Your only job now is to not break the chain."**

Sounds easy enough, right? Simple, yet effective. So hang a big calendar on your wall in a spot where you'll see it every day, designate a "habit marker," and place a big "X" on each day when you engage in your habit. Once you've got a good winning streak going, you'll be surprised how motivated you feel to keep the chain intact.

Although it's simple, I've found this technique to be very effective in my own efforts to write on a daily basis. Because I can visually see every day I skip, the calendar actually makes me uncomfortable with my procrastination. This pushes me even further to get motivated and write.

IN A NUTSHELL:

- Step 1: Choose your keystone habit
- Step 2: Create a small habit
- Step 3: Choose your reward
- Step 4: Use an "if-then" strategy
- Step 5: Be a realistic-optimist
- Step 6: Recruit an accountability partner
- Step 7: Shape your environment to encourage the behavior
- Step 8: Create a chain

Chapter 12

...AND THEN YOU FALL

Okay, so you've got the first eight steps under your belt no problem—you chose a keystone habit, picked out a few small habits, chose a reward, established an "if-then" strategy, adopted a "realistic optimist" mindset, picked an accountability partner, perfected your environment, and even got a solid start on creating a chain of successful days on your handy wall calendar.

But remember, the steps themselves don't guarantee success on a day-to-day basis. There are bound to be times when you fail to engage in your chosen habits, and that is okay! Nobody's perfect, and it's important that you don't expect yourself to be either. **This doesn't mean you should hold yourself to a lower standard; it just means you should set some realistic expectations.**

So when the day comes when you inevitably fall just sort of success, avoid giving up at all costs! Get back up, realize that failure and success (hopefully more of the latter) are both important parts of the habit formation process, and start building another chain. This time, make it your goal to build an even bigger chain than you did before, and let the anticipation of an even longer chain motivate you.

I never said habit formation would be easy, and I'm not about to now—it takes plenty of time and persistence to successfully build a new habit into your daily routine. Just like a child learning how to ride a bicycle, you too will fall off (so to speak). But instead of giving up, use your failures as a learning opportunity. Then brush yourself off, get back out there, and persist.

The habit formation concepts and steps for success that we've discussed throughout this book will be instrumental in making behavioral change more manageable. Before you know it, after committing just 10 minutes per day to completing the small habits you've selected, you will have paved the way for some major transformation in your life.

IN A NUTSHELL:

- Step 1: Choose your keystone habit
- Step 2: Create a small habit
- Step 3: Choose your reward
- Step 4: Use an "if-then" strategy
- Step 5: Be a realistic-optimist
- Step 6: Recruit an accountability partner
- Step 7: Shape your environment to encourage the behavior
- Step 8: Create a chain
- Step 9: Persist at it

Free Bonus:
The 9-Step Habit Worksheet

REMINDER: If you haven't already, be sure to grab the two-page *9-Step Habit Worksheet* which will help you immediately put these tools into practice.

Even if you don't take advantage of any of the other resources, take advantage of this one. But don't just download it, PRINT IT, <u>use it</u> and you'll begin to notice remarkable changes in your life.
www.AkashKaria.com/Habits

Chapter 13

WRAP UP

Congratulations! If you've successfully implemented the steps in this book, you've probably made transformations not only in the habit chosen, but also in other unrelated areas of your life (that's the power of keystone habits). In fact, you may even be surprised by how quickly you've made these changes (that's the power of small habits).

The power of small habits combined with keystone habits has the potential to transform your physical, emotional, and financial destiny. I know because I've seen witnessed this incredible power in my own life as well as in the lives of the clients I coach.

Even though this is a short book, we've packed in a lot of high-impact ideas, so in this chapter I want to summarize the most important ones. You can keep referring back to them as you progress on your personal development journey:

- The trouble with lofty goals like promotions, massive weight loss, and getting out of debt is that they often require major changes to our existing habits.

- Our habits that have been so programmed in our neurological pathways that we don't even know they exist.

- Increase your chances of success by decreasing the scale of your undertaking. Instead of pursuing a lofty goal, focus on establishing small habits instead.

- Small habits are those habits that are so small that they take very little willpower to carry out and thus make achieving them very likely.

- Small habits remove the willpower issue from the equation, allow you to experience small wins, and generate momentum that keep you motivated.

- Keystone habits are those habits that set off a chain reaction of new and improved behaviors in other unrelated areas. They are a powerful tool for personal transformation.

Some examples of keystone habits include exercising, making your bed, food journaling, and tracking your income and expenses.

- Keystone habits work for individuals as well as organizations. For example, Paul O'Neill, the new CEO of the Aluminum Company of America, focused on an organizational keystone habit (worker safety, in his case) to increase annual net income by 500%.

- Small Habits + Keystone Habits = Big Results.

- According to research, a new behavior can take anywhere from 18 to 254 days to become a habit. The average timeframe for habit formation, according to the study by Dr. Phillippa Lally, is 66 days, so don't give up too early. Choose your keystone habit, break it down into a small habit, and commit to performing it every day for 66 days.

- To increase your motivation, focus on the "big picture." Rather than dwelling on any inconvenience involved in performing your small habits, dwell on the overall outcome you are hoping to achieve. Say it out loud if you have to, because this big-picture thinking can be a strong motivational tool to have in your toolbox.

- People are driven by pain and pleasure. If you associate enough pleasure to taking action on your habit and enough pain to not taking action, then you'll be successful.

- To associate pleasure to completing your habit:
  o Find ways to make it fun.
  o Choose a reward you enjoy and tie it to the completion of the habit.

- To associate pain to not taking action on your habit:
  o Withhold the reward when you fail to take action.
  o Penalize failure by tying a consequence to failure to take action.

- Use the if-then strategy to triple your chances of following through on your daily habit. In one research study focused on participants who were attempting to establish a regular exercise routine, 91% of participants who used if-then planning were successful as compared to only 39% of those who did no such planning.

- Avoid negative if-then plans because they focus your attention on the action you are hoping to avoid.

- Be confident about your ability to achieve your goal: One study that focused on the performance of sales personnel at one organization found that those who scored high on an optimism test upon joining the sales team actually sold 37% more product in their first two years than their coworkers.

- However, positive thinking alone does have its downside: Positive thinking fools our minds into perceiving that we've already attained our goal, slackening our readiness to pursue it.

- The solution? Be a realistic optimist! Think positively about the future while still recognizing any barriers that may stand in your way.

- Use mental contrasting to increase your chances of success: Visualize success, but imagine the obstacles and come up with solutions.

- Write down your small + keystone habit goal. A study conducted at Dominican University found that people who put their goals in writing were able to achieve about 50% more than their peers with non-written goals. The study also found that participants who wrote down their goals were even more successful when they publicly broke down their goals into further actionable commitments and were held accountable by a friend via weekly progress reports.

- When choosing an accountability partner, choose someone who has characteristics and behavioral patterns that you wish to emulate.

- Shape your environment for success. Pay close attention to the factors in your environment that motivate or distract you. If you're struggling to cement a new habit in your daily routine, consider changing something about your current environment to make it more enjoyable to you.

- Use the Seinfeld calendar to track your progress. As comedian Jerry Seinfeld says, "You'll like seeing that chain, especially when you get a few weeks under your belt. Your only job now is to not break the chain."

- Persist: As clichéd as it sounds, don't give up! Keep pursuing your new habit until it becomes automatic and your day doesn't feel complete without it.

I encourage you to continue using the principles you've learned to design the life you deserve! Keep stacking more great habits on top of the ones you've already mastered in order to live out your true greatness.

To your best life,

Akash Karia

QUESTIONS OR COMMENTS?

I'd love to hear your thoughts. Email me on:
Akash@AkashKaria.com/ akash.speaker@gmail.com

INTERESTED IN HAVING ME SPEAK AT YOUR NEXT EVENT?

I deliver high-impact keynotes and workshops on productivity, time management, success psychology and effective communication.

Check out the full list of my training programs and keynotes on www.AkashKaria.com/Keynotesand reach me on akash.speaker@gmail.com to discuss how we can work together.

GRAB $297 WORTH OF FREE RESOURCES

Want to learn the small but powerful hacks to make you insanely productive?

Want to discover the scientifically proven techniques to ignite your influence?

Interested in mastering the art of public speaking and charisma?

Then head over to www.AkashKaria.com to grab your free "Success Toolkit" (free MP3s, eBooks and videos designed to unleash your excellence). Be sure to sign up for the newsletter and join over 15,200 of your peers to receive free, exclusive content that I don't share on my blog.

YOU MIGHT ALSO ENJOY

If you enjoyed this book, then check out:

EMOTIONAL HABITS: THE 7 THINGS RESILIENT PEOPLE DO DIFFERENTLY

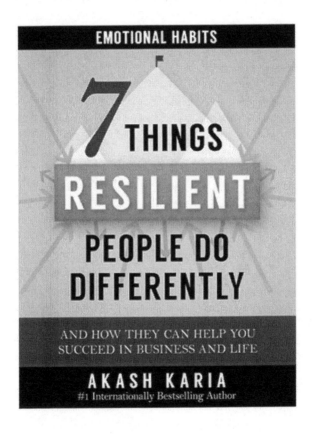

http://viewbook.at/7resilience

"...**a quick read that can have immediate and long term benefits.** The exercises in chapter two are really good. The advice in chapters 3 and 4 is spot on. I'm going to share it with my three sons."
~ Phil Barth

"...**a great book** if you're looking to master your emotions, become more resilient, flexible, and ultimately successful..."
~ M. Sean Marshall

*

New research reveals that resilience – more than IQ – is a key factor in determining your success and well-being, at work as well as in your relationships.

In fact, studies show that people with higher levels of resilience have higher productivity, better health, greater morale, higher job satisfaction and lower stress.

DISCOVER 7 SCIENCE-BACKED TOOLS THAT MAKE THE DIFFERENCE WHEN IT COUNTS

In this book, you will discover the 7 things resilient people do differently...and how to apply them in your own life so that you can:

- **Persevere through adversity.**

- Quickly bounce back from disappointments.

- **Break negative emotional patterns by taking control of your self-talk and inner movies.**

- Instantly shift your emotional state using the power of physiology.

- **Create greater drive and ambition by mastering the use of self-directed questions.**

- Supercharge your energy levels at a moment's notice.

- **Experience even greater excitement, passion, happiness and fulfillment in every area of your life.**

Using the 7 habits of resilient people discussed in this book, you will be able to handle the vulnerabilities of intimate relationships, the risks and failures of business and the ups and downs of life.

Just one idea in this book might be what you need.

"I'll definitely be reading this book again, because I spent the whole time analyzing my own thoughts and reactions and found a great deal to work on."
~ Rebecca Vickers

"[Akash] has knocked it out of the park... A great read full of examples...Highly recommended."
~ Jamie Hill

Ready to get started?

Then grab the book here:
http://viewbook.at/7resilience

CONNECT WITH AKASH

Grab your Free Success Toolkit:
www.AkashKaria.com/Free

Check out more Great books:
http://viewauthor.at/Akash

Email for Speaking/Training Inquires:
akash@akashkaria.com / akash.speaker@gmail.com

Connect on LinkedIn:
www.LinkedIn.com/In/AkashKaria

Made in the USA
Lexington, KY
29 December 2016